HERCULES

THE TWELVE LABORS

A GREEK MYTH

STORY BY
PAUL STORRIE
PENCILS BY
STEVE KURTH
INKS BY
BARBARA SCHULZ

1 NEMEA (LION)
2 LERNEA (HYDRA)
3 CERYNEA (HIND)
4 MOUNT ERYMANTHUS (BOAR)
5 ELIS (AUGEAN STABLES)
6 LAKE STYMPHALIS (BIRDS)
7 CRETE (CRETAN BULL)
8 THRACE (DIOMEDES' HORSES)
9 LAND OF THE AMAZONS (HIPPOLYTA'S BELT)*
10 ERYTHEIA (GERYON'S CATTLE)
11 GARDEN OF THE HESPERIDES (GOLDEN APPLES)*
12 HADES (CERBERUS THE THREE-HEADED DOG)*

* THE LOCATIONS OF THESE LEGENDARY SITES ARE THE BEST ESTIMATES OF HISTORIANS.

HERCULES

THE TWELVE LABORS

A GREEK MYTH

GREECE
MOUNT OLYMPUS
DELPHI
THEBES
MYCENAE
MEDITERRANEAN SEA
AFRICA
1 2 3 4 5 6 7 8 9 12

GRAPHIC UNIVERSE™ • MINNEAPOLIS

The character Hercules may or may not have been based on an actual person. Regardless, the stories of his great feats of strength, courage, and resourcefulness are among the most famous Greek legends. The Greeks called their greatest hero Herakles. But the Romans knew him as Hercules. This latter title has come down through the ages as the most popular name for this larger-than-life figure. To create the story of Hercules' Twelve Labors, author Paul Storrie relied heavily on both Thomas Bulfinch's *The Age of Fable*, first published in 1859, and Edith Hamilton's *Mythology*, first published in 1942. Both of these drew their material from the work of ancient poets such as Ovid and Virgil. Artist Steve Kurth used numerous historical and traditional sources to give the art an authentic feel, from the classical Greek architecture to the clothing, weapons and armor worn by the characters.

STORY BY PAUL STORRIE

PENCILS BY STEVE KURTH
INKS BY BARBARA SCHULZ

COLORING BY HI-FI DESIGN

LETTERING BY BILL HAUSER

Graphic Universe™
A division of Lerner Publishing Group, Inc.
241 First Avenue North
Minneapolis, MN 55401 USA

For reading levels and more information, look up this title at www.lernerbooks.com.

Library of Congress Cataloging-in-Publication Data

Storrie, Paul D.
Hercules : the Twelve Labors / by Paul Storrie ; illustrations by Steve Kurth.
p. cm. — (Graphic myths and legends)
ISBN 978-0-8225-3084-8 (lib. bdg. : alk. paper)
ISBN 978-0-8225-7214-5 (eb pdf)
1. Heracles (Greek mythology)—Juvenile literature. I. Kurth, Steve. II. Title. III. Series: Graphic myths and legends (Minneapolis, Minn.)
BL820.H5S86 2007
398.2'0938'02—dc22 2005023617

Manufactured in the United States of America
10 - 43960 - 3789 - 10/23/2019

TABLE OF CONTENTS

THE LEGEND BEGINS
LONG AGO, IN THE FAR OFF LAND OF GREECE, THERE LIVED A HERO NAMED HERCULES. THERE HAS NEVER BEEN A MAN AS STRONG, BEFORE OR SINCE.
HIS MOTHER WAS ALCMENA, A MORTAL, BUT HIS FATHER WAS ZEUS, THE KING OF THE GODS.
THE GODDESS HERA WAS JEALOUS THAT ZEUS, HER HUSBAND, LOVED A MORTAL WOMAN. BECAUSE OF THAT, SHE HATED HERCULES.

HERCULES WAS RAISED IN THE CITY OF THEBES, ALONG WITH HIS HALF BROTHER, IPHICLES.
EACH NIGHT, ALCMENA WOULD PUT HER SONS TO BED IN A GREAT BRONZE SHIELD THAT SERVED AS THEIR CRIB.
ONE NIGHT, HERA SENT TWO SERPENTS TO SLAY THE SLEEPING HERCULES, NOT CARING THAT HIS BROTHER WAS IN DANGER TOO.
BUT ZEUS WATCHED OVER HIS SON AND SENT A BRIGHT LIGHT TO WAKE HIM.
EVEN AS A CHILD, HE WAS STRONG ENOUGH TO SAVE HIS BROTHER AND HIMSELF.
WHEN HE WAS A GROWN MAN, HE WENT TO THE ORACLE AT DELPHI, WHO GAVE MESSAGES FROM THE GODS, TO LEARN WHAT HE SHOULD DO WITH HIS GREAT GIFT OF STRENGTH.
SON OF ZEUS, YOU MUST GO TO YOUR COUSIN, KING EURYSTHEUS OF MYCENAE, AND PUT YOURSELF IN HIS SERVICE.
THIS IS THE WILL OF THE GODS.
THOUGH HERCULES COULD NOT SEE HER, IT WAS THE GODDESS HERA WHO SPOKE THROUGH THE ORACLE THAT DAY.

FANTASTIC CREATURES
THE JOURNEY TO MYCENAE WAS LONG, BUT HERCULES LOOKED FORWARD TO SEEING HIS COUSIN.
WHAT HE DID NOT KNOW WAS THAT KING EURYSTHEUS WAS JEALOUS OF HIS STRENGTH AND FAME.
SO, HERCULES, YOU SAY THE GODS SENT YOU TO SERVE ME?
WELL THEN, WE SHALL HAVE TO FIND LABORS EQUAL TO YOUR AMAZING STRENGTH.
THE KING DID NOT KNOW THAT THE QUIET WORDS THAT CAME TO HIM WERE WHISPERED BY JEALOUS HERA, HOPING TO DO HERCULES HARM.
YES ... YES.
IN NEMEA, BY THE SACRED GROVE OF ZEUS,
A FIERCE LION IS MENACING THE COUNTRYSIDE.
I MUST WARN YOU, NO HUNTER OR HERO HAS BEEN ABLE TO KILL IT.
THE CREATURE'S SKIN RESISTS EVERY WEAPON.

HERCULES SOON ARRIVED IN NEMEA TO BEGIN HIS FIRST LABOR. IT WAS NOT LONG BEFORE HE FOUND SIGNS OF HIS PREY.
I HOPE YOU ENJOYED YOUR MEAL, MONSTER.
IT WILL BE YOUR LAST!
RRROOOOAAARR!!
BUT MY CLUB WILL...
YOUR HIDE IS AS TOUGH AS RUMORS SAY!

WHAM!
...STRIKE YOU DOWN!
PERHAPS NOT.
IF WEAPONS FAIL...
MY STRENGTH WILL HAVE TO BE ENOUGH!

HAS THERE BEEN NO WORD?
SURELY THE BEAST HAS DEVOURED HIM BY NOW.
NO WORD YET MY KING, BUT...
EURYSTHEUS!
AAAHHH!
HA, HA, HA! HA!
NO NEED FOR FEAR, COUSIN!
DO YOU LIKE MY NEW CLOAK? IT WAS NOT EASY TO GET.
THE KING WAS ASHAMED THAT THE SIGHT OF HERCULES IN THE LION'S SKIN HAD FRIGHTENED HIM. HE WANTED TO MAKE HERCULES PAY FOR THAT EMBARRASSMENT.
YES, VERY NICE. PERHAPS IT WILL HELP PROTECT YOU DURING YOUR NEXT TASK.
IN THE SWAMPS OF LERNEA, THERE LIVES A BEAST CALLED THE HYDRA...

TO BEGIN HIS SECOND LABOR AS SOON AS POSSIBLE, HERCULES ASKED HIS NEPHEW IOLAUS TO TAKE HIM TO LERNEA BY CHARIOT. IOLAUS WAS THE SON OF IPHICLES, HERCULES' HALF BROTHER.
MUCH BETTER. HARD TO FIGHT WHAT YOU CAN BARELY SEE.
IS IT TRUE THAT THIS HYDRA HAS NINE HEADS, HERCULES? AND THAT ONE OF THE HEADS CANNOT BE KILLED?
SO EURYSTHEUS TELLS ME. AND THAT ITS BLOOD IS POISON.
I WONDER IF THERE WAS ANYTHING HE DECIDED NOT TO TELL?
LET'S SEE IF WE CAN ROUSE THE BEAST.
HISsSSSsSSSssSSSSSSSSSSSSSSSSSSSSSSSSSSSs

THIS CANNOT BE!
EACH HEAD I DESTROY, TWO TAKE ITS PLACE!
IOLAUS!
GRAB A BRANCH FROM THE FIRE.
HURRY!
IOLAUS?
I UNDERSTAND!
TSSSSS!

WELL DONE! WE MAY WIN OUT AFTER ALL!
THE GRIM BATTLE CONTINUED AS DAYLIGHT FADED. THEN, ONLY ONE HEAD REMAINED. THE IMMORTAL ONE.
NOW, LET IT END!
AFTER HE STRUCK OFF THE IMMORTAL HEAD, HERCULES BURIED IT BENEATH A ROCK. THEN HE AND IOLAUS PREPARED TO RETURN TO MYCENAE.
IF THIS MONSTER'S BLOOD IS POISON, THESE ARROWS MAY PROVE USEFUL IN MY OTHER LABORS.

WHAT WERE YOU THINKING, HERCULES? TO TAKE A BOY HIS AGE INTO SUCH DANGER!
BESIDES, THE GODS' WISH WAS FOR YOU TO SERVE ME, NOT HAVE IOLAUS PERFORM YOUR LABORS FOR YOU!
HE ALREADY HAS A WARRIOR'S COURAGE. NOW HE MUST LEARN...
NO MATTER. YOUR THIRD LABOR WILL BE LESS CHALLENGING, SO YOU WILL HAVE NO NEED OF HELP.
I WANT YOU TO FETCH ME THE CERYNEAN HIND. AMAZING CREATURE -- IT HAS HORNS OF GOLD!
YOU WANT ME TO BRING YOU A DEER? HARDLY A LABOR TO MATCH MY PROWESS.
THIS SHOULD NOT TAKE LONG.
I ADMIT, I DO NOT UNDERSTAND EITHER. A HIND?
ONE SACRED TO THE MOON GODDESS ARTEMIS. IF HE KILLS IT, SHE WILL SURELY PUNISH HIM.
BUT YOU TOLD HIM...
I TOLD HIM TO FETCH THE ANIMAL, NOT HARM IT.
AH, YES. VERY CLEVER INDEED.

MONTHS LATER, HERCULES RETURNED.
EURYSTHEUS!
HERE IT IS!
HOW...? WHAT ABOUT...?
LONG MONTHS I TRACKED AND CHASED HER. SHE WAS FAST AND CLEVER. I THOUGHT I MIGHT NEVER CATCH HER.
FINALLY, I USED AN ARROW TO BRING HER DOWN.
THEN, AS I MADE MY WAY BACK, ARTEMIS APPEARED BEFORE ME!
SEEMS THIS GOLDEN-HORNED CREATURE IS A FAVORITE OF HERS.
SHE WAS ANGRY JUST THINKING THAT I HAD HURT IT.
HOW IS IT SHE LET YOU PASS, UNHINDERED AND UNHARMED?
LUCKY FOR ME, I HAD NOT HURT IT.
I KNEW SUCH A MAGNIFICENT CREATURE MUST BE TOUCHED BY THE GODS.
BUT YOU SAID...
THAT I BROUGHT IT DOWN WITH AN ARROW. I SHOT BETWEEN ITS LEGS AND TRIPPED IT. THEN I CAUGHT IT BEFORE IT COULD RUN.
SINCE IT WAS NOT HURT, ARTEMIS LET ME FINISH MY TASK. I HAD TO PROMISE TO LET IT GO. NOW I HAVE!

LATER...
WHAT TROUBLES YOU, MY KING?
Bah. IT IS ONLY A MATTER OF TIME BEFORE HERCULES RETURNS FROM HIS FOURTH LABOR.
SLAYING THE ERYMANTHEAN BOAR WILL BE NO CHALLENGE TO HIM.
PERHAPS NOT, MY KING.
BUT THE FEARSOME BOAR HAS BEEN TERRORIZING THOSE WHO LIVE NEAR MOUNT ERYMANTHUS.
AT LEAST IT WILL NO LONGER HURT YOUR PEOPLE.
TRUE. I JUST WISH I COULD THINK OF SOME OTHER LABOR TO...
KING EURYSTHEUS!
HERCULES IS COMING!
IT IS AMAZING, MY KING.
HE CHASED THE BEAST UP AND DOWN THE MOUNTAINSIDE FOR DAYS.
FINALLY, HE DROVE IT INTO A SNOWBANK NEAR THE PEAK.
THEN HE WAITED UNTIL IT WAS EXHAUSTED FROM STRUGGLING TO GET FREE!
EXHAUSTED?!? THEN IT IS STILL ALIVE?!?
Y-YES, MY KING.
AND HE IS BRINGING IT HERE?
YES, MY KING.
GO! RUN! TELL HERCULES THAT FROM NOW ON HE SHOULD SHOW THE PROOF OF HIS LABORS TO THE GUARD CAPTAIN AT THE GATE.
NOT TO ME, YOU UNDERSTAND? NOT TO ME!

GREAT CHALLENGES
KING EURYSTHEUS WAS ASHAMED AT BEING SO FRIGHTENED ABOUT THE BOAR. HE BLAMED HERCULES AND WANTED TO EMBARRASS HIS COUSIN JUST AS MUCH.
FOR THE FIFTH LABOR, EURYSTHEUS SENT HERCULES TO CLEAN OUT THE STABLES OF KING AUGEAS IN A SINGLE DAY, A TASK AS IMPOSSIBLE AS IT WAS DISGUSTING.
THERE THEY ARE -- THE STABLES THAT YOU AGREED TO CLEAN!
Ugh! BY THE SMELL, I CAN TELL NO ONE HAS TOUCHED THEM IN YEARS.
I WILL DO IT, BUT YOU MUST GIVE ME ONE OF EVERY TEN ANIMALS IN RETURN.
HA! WHY NOT?
TELL ME, PHYLEUS, MY SON, DO YOU THINK HE'LL MANAGE IT?
I DON'T KNOW, FATHER.

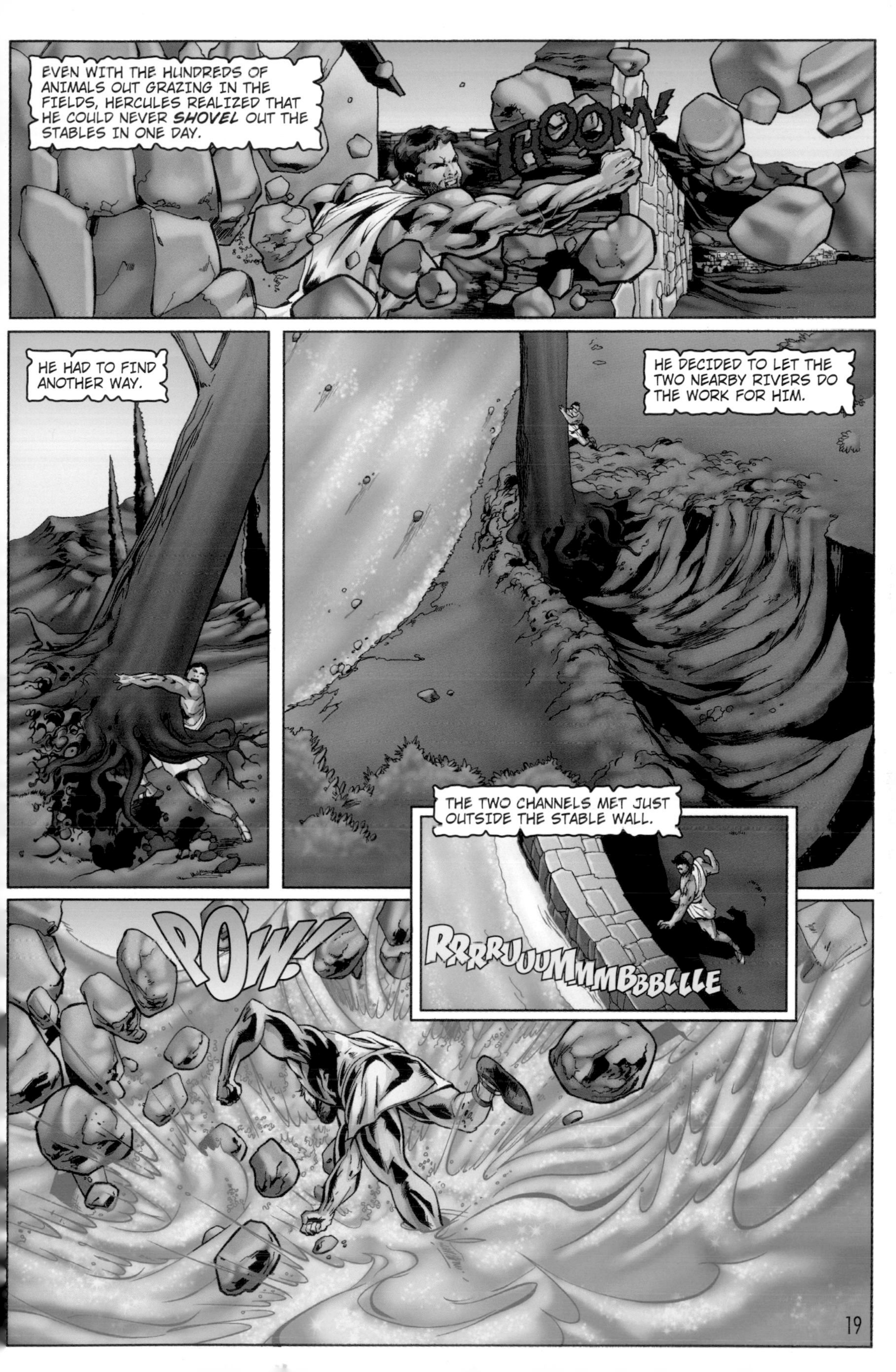
EVEN WITH THE HUNDREDS OF ANIMALS OUT GRAZING IN THE FIELDS, HERCULES REALIZED THAT HE COULD NEVER SHOVEL OUT THE STABLES IN ONE DAY.
THOOM!
HE HAD TO FIND ANOTHER WAY.
HE DECIDED TO LET THE TWO NEARBY RIVERS DO THE WORK FOR HIM.
THE TWO CHANNELS MET JUST OUTSIDE THE STABLE WALL.
RRRRUUUMMMMBBBLLLE
POW!

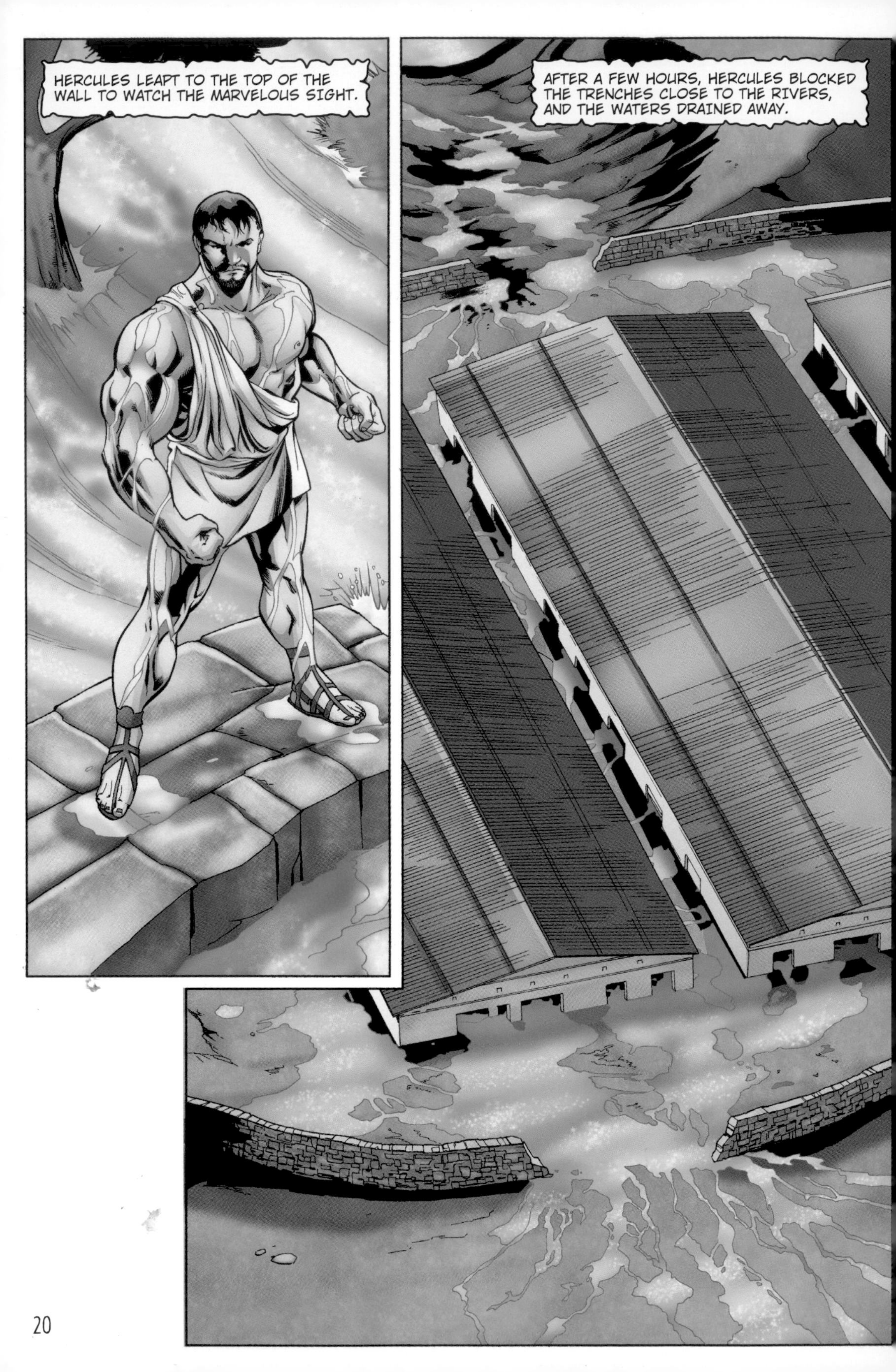
HERCULES LEAPT TO THE TOP OF THE WALL TO WATCH THE MARVELOUS SIGHT.
AFTER A FEW HOURS, HERCULES BLOCKED THE TRENCHES CLOSE TO THE RIVERS, AND THE WATERS DRAINED AWAY.

ARE YOU INSANE?!?
I HAVE DONE WHAT I SAID I WOULD DO. TIME TO PAY UP!
NO, IT IS NOT!
I HAVE LEARNED THAT YOU DID THIS AT THE BIDDING OF KING EURYSTHEUS AND THAT THE GODS TOLD YOU TO SERVE HIM. YOU HAD NO RIGHT TO ASK FOR PAYMENT!
WHATEVER HIS REASON, YOU PROMISED HIM THE ANIMALS, FATHER...
WHAT? YOU TAKE HIS SIDE?
GET OUT OF MY KINGDOM, THE PAIR OF YOU!
COUNT YOURSELVES LUCKY TO LEAVE WITH YOUR LIVES!
DON'T WORRY, PHYLEUS. YOU'VE DONE NOTHING WRONG. SOMEDAY, YOU WILL INHERIT THE KINGDOM AS YOU SHOULD.
FOR NOW, YOU MUST COME WITH ME TO MYCENAE. THE LOOK ON EURYSTHEUS'S FACE WHEN HE LEARNS I COMPLETED HIS TASK WITHOUT WADING IN FILTH WILL RAISE YOUR SPIRITS!

HERCULES WAS RIGHT ABOUT HIS COUSIN'S DISAPPOINTMENT. HE WAS NOT SURPRISED WHEN THE KING SENT HIM TO HIS SIXTH LABOR RIGHT AWAY, BUT HE WAS PUZZLED BY THE TASK.
KING EURYSTHEUS SENT HIM TO THE STYMPHALIAN LAKE TO CHASE AWAY SOME BIRDS THAT WERE BOTHERING THE FARMERS THERE. IT SEEMED TOO EASY.
WHEN HE ARRIVED, THE LAKESHORE LOOKED PEACEFUL.
HE DECIDED TO ASK ONE OF THE FARMERS MORE ABOUT THEIR PROBLEM.
I AM HERCULES. KING EURYSTHEUS HAS SENT ME TO DRIVE AWAY THE BIRDS.
QUICKLY! COME INSIDE.
WHY ARE YOUR ANIMALS IN HERE, INSTEAD OF THE PEN?
NOTHING IS SAFE OUTSIDE! THE BIRDS WOULD GET THEM.
THEY ARE MONSTERS! THEIR CLAWS AND BEAKS ARE MADE OF BRASS.
THEIR FEATHERS SHINE LIKE BRONZE AND DROP FROM THE SKY LIKE ARROWS!
WHAT THEY KILL, THEY DRAG AWAY TO EAT.
IT SEEMS EURYSTHEUS FORGOT TO TELL ME THE CREATURES WERE SO FIERCE.
NO MATTER. I WILL DRIVE THEM OFF.
NO! STAY!
FEAR NOT! YOUR WARNINGS SHOULD KEEP ME SAFE.

THIS SHOULD ROUSE THEM.
CLANG!
CLANG!
CLANG!
CLANG!
AH! HERE THEY COME.
CLANG!
CLANG!
CLANG!
TAK TAK TAK TAK TAK TAK TAK TAK TAK TAK TAK TAK TAK TAK
ENOUGH OF THIS!
ARRGH!

KREEEE!
THUNK!
WHISSSSH
BECAUSE OF THE HYDRA'S BLOOD ON THE ARROWS, A SCRATCH WAS ENOUGH TO KILL.
THUMP
THUMP
HERCULES FIRED ARROW AFTER ARROW.
KREEEE!
HIS ONLY FEAR WAS THAT HE WOULD NOT HAVE ENOUGH.
EVENTUALLY, THE LAST FEW BIRDS FLEW OFF. WHAT HAPPENED TO THEM, NO ONE KNOWS, BUT THEY NEVER RETURNED TO THE STYMPHALIAN LAKE AGAIN.

EXTRAORDINARY PRIZES
FOR HIS SEVENTH LABOR, KING EURYSTHEUS SENT HERCULES TO THE ISLAND OF CRETE TO STEAL A MIRACULOUS WHITE BULL. IT HAD BEEN GIVEN TO KING MINOS, THE RULER THERE, BY THE SEA GOD POSEIDON.
MINOS WAS SUPPOSED TO SACRIFICE THE BULL, BUT IT WAS SO BEAUTIFUL THAT HE SACRIFICED ANOTHER BULL INSTEAD.
YOU LOOK UNHAPPY, HERCULES.
I DO NOT LIKE THE IDEA OF BECOMING A THIEF, CAPTAIN, BUT I HAVE NO CHOICE.
I MUST DO AS YOUR KING, EURYSTHEUS, COMMANDS.
BEFORE LONG, HERCULES FOUND SOMEONE WHO COULD HELP HIM FIND THE BULL.
YOU MAY FIND THE BEAST IN THAT DIRECTION, BUT I WOULD NOT SEEK IT.
WHEN KING MINOS DID NOT SACRIFICE IT, THE SEA GOD DROVE IT MAD.
NOW IT KILLS ANYONE WHO COMES CLOSE.
ANOTHER DANGER THAT EURYSTHEUS DID NOT WARN ME ABOUT!
I AM BEGINNING TO THINK HE MAY NOT LIKE ME.

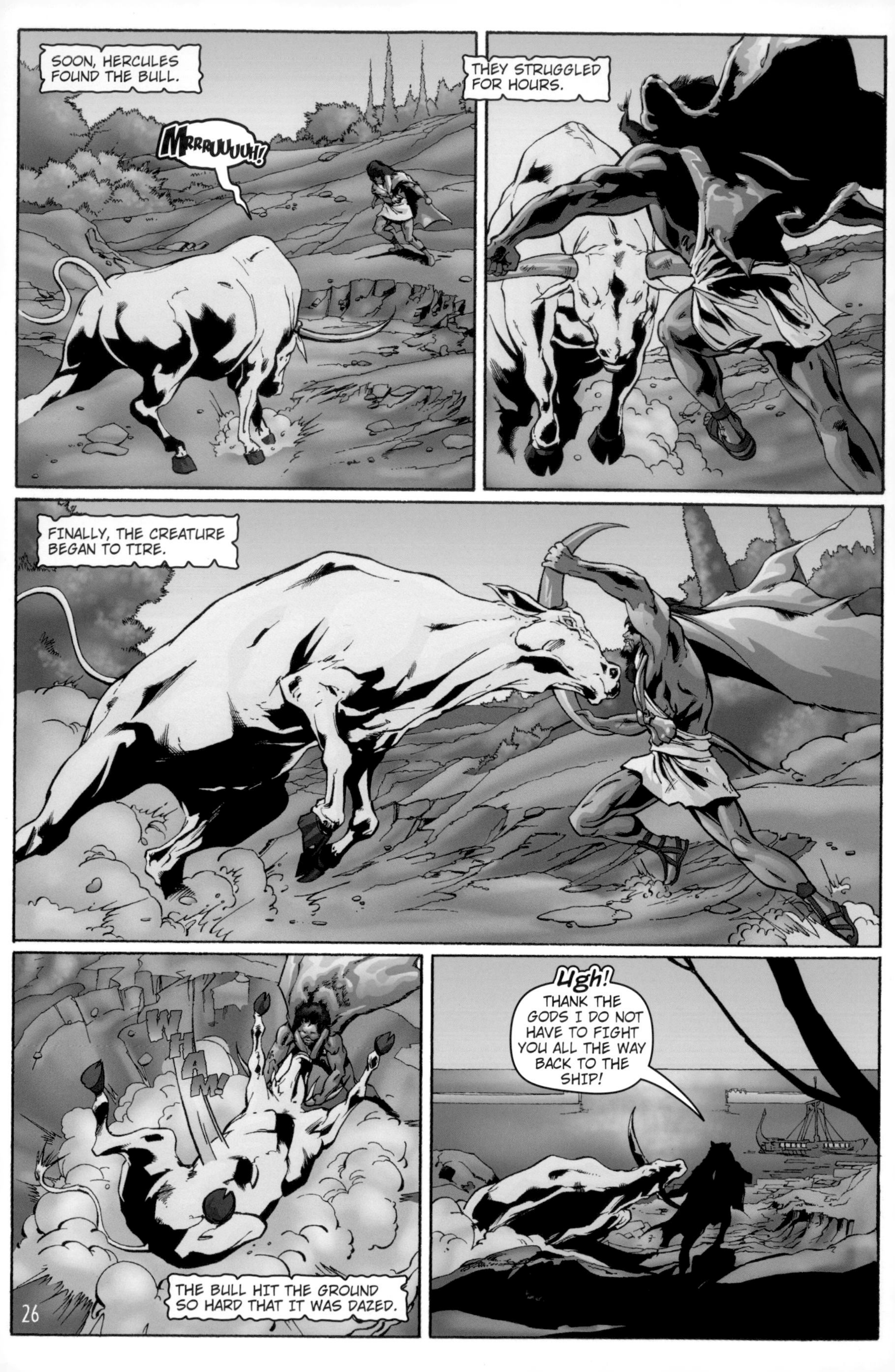
SOON, HERCULES FOUND THE BULL.
MRRRUUUUH!
THEY STRUGGLED FOR HOURS.
FINALLY, THE CREATURE BEGAN TO TIRE.
WHAM!
THE BULL HIT THE GROUND SO HARD THAT IT WAS DAZED.
Ugh!
THANK THE GODS I DO NOT HAVE TO FIGHT YOU ALL THE WAY BACK TO THE SHIP!

AFTER HERCULES DELIVERED THE WHITE BULL OF CRETE, KING EURYSTHEUS SENT HIM TO THRACE TO STEAL AWAY A PAIR OF PRIZE MARES OWNED BY KING DIOMEDES. HIS *EIGHTH LABOR* SOUNDED EASY ENOUGH, BUT HERCULES HAD LEARNED TO EXPECT UNPLEASANT SURPRISES.
GREETINGS, FRIEND!
ARE THESE THE STABLES OF KING DIOMEDES?
YES, THEY ARE. YOU MUST NOT BE FROM THRACE. ALL THE LOCALS STAY AWAY.
WHY IS THAT? I HEAR THE MARES THAT DRAW THE KING'S CHARIOT ARE AMAZING CREATURES.
SO YOU CAME TO SEE THEM?
INDEED I DID.
SORRY, BUT THAT WOULD NOT BE SAFE. TRUST ME, I AM THEIR TRAINER.
YOU SOUND UNHAPPY ABOUT IT.
THE KING LIKES THEM TRAINED AND FED A CERTAIN WAY. IT MAKES THEM DANGEROUS.
FOR EXAMPLE, MOST HORSES LIKE TO BE PETTED. THESE WOULD HAPPILY GNAW YOUR HAND OFF.
GOOD TO KNOW.
TO BE HONEST, I WAS SENT HERE TO STEAL THEM.
I DID NOT LIKE THE IDEA, BUT IT SOUNDS LIKE DIOMEDES IS NOT FIT TO OWN THEM. I HOPE YOU WILL NOT TRY TO STOP ME.
I DOUBT I COULD, EVEN IF I WANTED TO. GOOD LUCK TO YOU. THEY WILL BE BETTER OFF AWAY FROM HERE.

CRUNCH!
THE TWO OF YOU ARE EVERY BIT AS NASTY AS YOUR TRAINER SAYS!
CLACK!
CLACK!
SETTLE DOWN. YOU WILL GET NO TASTE OF ME.
THIEF!

THEY CAN HAVE YOU WHEN I FINISH!
TO DEFEND HIMSELF, HERCULES WAS FORCED TO RELEASE THE MARES.
No.
NOOOOOOOOOOOOOOOO!
SORRY. HE STRUCK ME WHEN I TRIED TO STOP HIM.
NO MATTER. IN THE END, HE GOT WHAT HE DESERVED.
PERHAPS. WILL EURYSTHEUS TREAT THEM BETTER?
I WILL TELL HIM WHAT HAPPENED TO DIOMEDES. IF I KNOW EURYSTHEUS, HE WILL BE TOO FRIGHTENED TO BE CRUEL TO THEM.

WHAT NOW? HERCULES HAS SUCCEEDED AT EVERY TASK I GAVE HIM. NOTHING HURTS HIM. NOTHING SHAMES HIM.
BUT WHAT...
YES! CALL FOR HERCULES!
FOR THE NINTH LABOR, KING EURYSTHEUS SENT HERCULES TO THE LAND OF THE AMAZONS. THE AMAZONS WERE A NATION OF FIERCE WARRIOR WOMEN WHO COULD FIGHT AS WELL AS ANY MAN. THE BRAVEST OF THEM, HIPPOLYTA, WAS THEIR QUEEN.
WHAT IS YOUR PURPOSE HERE?
I MUST SPEAK WITH HIPPOLYTA.
WHETHER YOU DO OR NOT WILL BE UP TO THE QUEEN.
I WILL BRING HER YOUR REQUEST.
UNTIL I RETURN, STAY ON YOUR SHIP.
IF YOU TRY TO COME ON LAND, MY COMRADES WILL STOP YOU.

A SHORT TIME LATER, THE QUEEN ARRIVED.
HAIL, HIPPOLYTA, QUEEN OF THE AMAZONS!
HAIL, HERCULES, HERO OF THEBES. WHY HAVE YOU MADE THE LONG JOURNEY TO MY LAND?
BY THE GODS' WILL, I SERVE MY COUSIN, KING EURYSTHEUS OF MYCENAE.
HE HAS COMMANDED THAT I BRING HIM THE GOLDEN BELT YOU WEAR.
YOU PLAN TO TAKE IT FROM ME? DO YOU THINK I WILL NOT FIGHT TO KEEP IT?
IT WAS A GIFT FROM ARES, THE GOD OF WAR.
I HOPE TO PERSUADE YOU TO PART WITH IT. I RESPECT YOU AND YOUR WARRIORS.
I DO NOT WISH TO BE YOUR ENEMY.
HAD YOU TRIED TO TAKE IT, I WOULD NEVER HAVE GIVEN IT UP.
BECAUSE YOU ASKED AND BECAUSE OF THE RESPECT I HAVE FOR YOU AND YOUR ADVENTURES,
I WILL GIVE IT TO YOU AS A TOKEN OF FRIENDSHIP.

ONCE AGAIN, HERA WAS NEARBY, WATCHING AND HOPING THAT HERCULES WOULD FAIL. WHEN SHE SAW THE QUEEN GIVE UP THE BELT WITHOUT A FIGHT, HERA DISGUISED HERSELF AS AN AMAZON TO MAKE TROUBLE.
LOOK! HERCULES MUST HAVE TAKEN THE QUEEN HOSTAGE!
WHY ELSE WOULD SHE SURRENDER SUCH A TREASURE?
YES! YOU MUST BE RIGHT!
WE MUST STOP THEM BEFORE THEY SET SAIL!
STOP THEM!!!
ATTACK!!!
WHAT IS THIS?!? YOU SPEAK OF FRIENDSHIP AND THEN YOUR WARRIORS ATTACK?
MY WARRIORS WOULD ONLY ATTACK IF THEY SAW SOME TREACHERY!
I SHOULD HAVE KNOWN BETTER THAN TO TRUST A MAN!
SAVE THE QUEEN!
GET THEM!
STOP THEM!!

SURRENDER NOW AND STOP THIS MADNESS!
SURRENDER?
NEVER!
oof!
YOU WANT YOUR QUEEN?
YOU CAN HAVE HER!
HURRY, MEN! WE GOT WHAT WE CAME FOR!
AGAIN I AM A THIEF FOR EURYSTHEUS.
I LIKE IT LESS EVERY TIME.

AS SOON AS HERCULES RETURNED WITH HIPPOLYTA'S GOLDEN BELT, KING EURYSTHEUS IMMEDIATELY SENT HIM ON ANOTHER JOURNEY.
WHAT TROUBLES YOU, HERCULES?
FOR MY TENTH LABOR, EURYSTHEUS SENDS ME TO STEAL. AGAIN.
THIS TIME WE TRAVEL TO ERYTHEIA, AN ISLAND FAR TO THE WEST.
I AM TO BRING BACK THE CATTLE OF SOMEONE CALLED GERYON.
WHEN HERCULES CAME TO THE END OF THE MEDITERRANEAN SEA, HE FOUND THE PASSAGE TOO NARROW AND ROCKY TO SAIL THROUGH.
HE PILED SOME OF THE ROCKS THAT BLOCKED HIS WAY INTO MOUNTAINS ON EITHER SIDE OF THE PASSAGE. TO THIS DAY, THEY ARE KNOWN AS THE PILLARS OF HERCULES.
WHEN THEY ARRIVED ON THE ISLAND, HERCULES WENT TO FIND THE CATTLE.
OUR LOOKOUT HAS JUST REPORTED THAT HERCULES IS COMING.
HE HAS THE CATTLE.
FINE. TELL THE MEN TO GET READY TO BRING THEM ABOARD.

WHEN HERCULES RETURNED, HE LOADED ALL THE CATTLE ONTO THE SHIP BY HIMSELF.
I DID NOT SEE HIM, BUT THE LOCALS TELL ME THIS GERYON IS SOME KIND OF MONSTER.
IT MAKES ME FEEL A LITTLE BETTER ABOUT TAKING HIS CATTLE FOR EURYSTHEUS.
RRRAAAAAAARRRRR!!
YOU'VE TAKEN MY CATTLE!
I'LL KILL YOU ALL!!
CRACK!
CRACK!
GET MY BOW! NOW!

NOOoOOOo!!!!
WHIST
ARRGGHHH!
YOU KILLED HIM WITH A POISONED ARROW? I AM SURPRISED, HERCULES.
YOU ARE A MIGHTY WARRIOR. WHY NOT FIGHT IT FAIRLY?
I THOUGHT ABOUT IT. THEN IT OCCURRED TO ME THAT YOU, YOUR CREW, AND YOUR SHIP MIGHT GET SMASHED TO PIECES IN THE FIGHT.
oh.

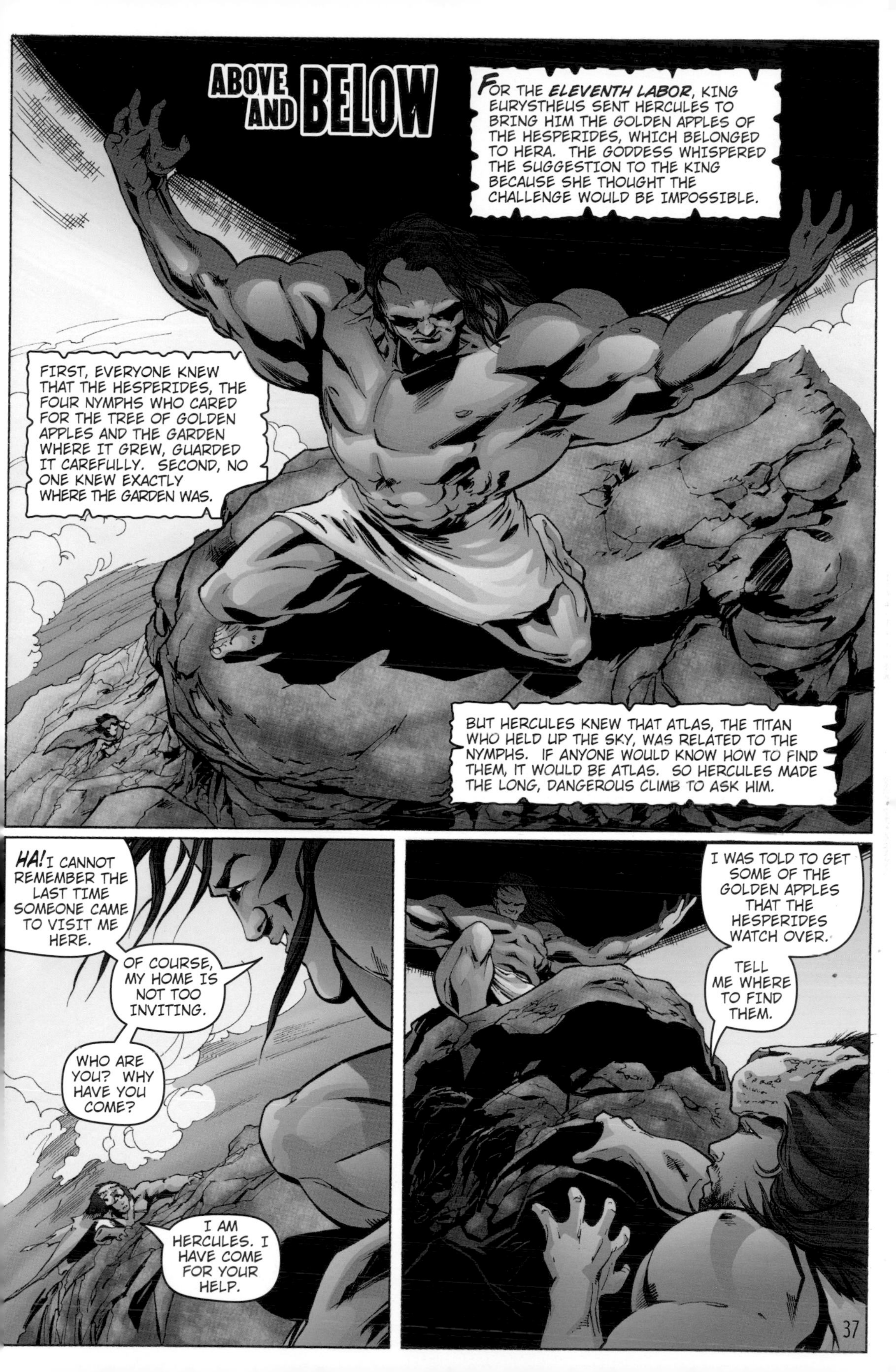
ABOVE AND BELOW
FOR THE ELEVENTH LABOR, KING EURYSTHEUS SENT HERCULES TO BRING HIM THE GOLDEN APPLES OF THE HESPERIDES, WHICH BELONGED TO HERA. THE GODDESS WHISPERED THE SUGGESTION TO THE KING BECAUSE SHE THOUGHT THE CHALLENGE WOULD BE IMPOSSIBLE.
FIRST, EVERYONE KNEW THAT THE HESPERIDES, THE FOUR NYMPHS WHO CARED FOR THE TREE OF GOLDEN APPLES AND THE GARDEN WHERE IT GREW, GUARDED IT CAREFULLY. SECOND, NO ONE KNEW EXACTLY WHERE THE GARDEN WAS.
BUT HERCULES KNEW THAT ATLAS, THE TITAN WHO HELD UP THE SKY, WAS RELATED TO THE NYMPHS. IF ANYONE WOULD KNOW HOW TO FIND THEM, IT WOULD BE ATLAS. SO HERCULES MADE THE LONG, DANGEROUS CLIMB TO ASK HIM.
HA! I CANNOT REMEMBER THE LAST TIME SOMEONE CAME TO VISIT ME HERE.
OF COURSE, MY HOME IS NOT TOO INVITING.
WHO ARE YOU? WHY HAVE YOU COME?
I AM HERCULES. I HAVE COME FOR YOUR HELP.
I WAS TOLD TO GET SOME OF THE GOLDEN APPLES THAT THE HESPERIDES WATCH OVER.
TELL ME WHERE TO FIND THEM.

HA, HA, HA! HA! HA!
YOU LAUGH AT ME?
NO, NO. DO NOT BE ANGRY. I JUST KNOW SOME THINGS THAT YOU DO NOT.
YOU SEE, EVEN IF I TOLD YOU WHERE THE GARDEN IS AND YOU GOT PAST THE HESPERIDES, THERE IS ANOTHER OBSTACLE.
A DRAGON. SOME SAY IT HAS ONE HUNDRED HEADS. NOW, EVEN I HAVE HEARD STORIES OF YOUR STRENGTH. I KNOW YOU BEAT THE HYDRA'S NINE HEADS.
BUT ONE HUNDRED? THAT MIGHT BE TOO MUCH, EVEN FOR YOU.
LET US MAKE A BARGAIN. IF I GO TO THE GARDEN, THE HESPERIDES WILL SURELY GIVE ME SOME APPLES AND THE DRAGON WILL LET THEM.
IF YOU HOLD UP THE SKY FOR ME A WHILE, I PROMISE I WILL BRING THE APPLES HERE TO YOU.
I'M SURE YOU'RE STRONG ENOUGH.
OF COURSE I AM!
JUST EASE YOUR BACK AGAINST IT AND TAKE THE WEIGHT FROM MY SHOULDERS.
VERY GOOD. I KNEW YOU COULD MANAGE.
Umph! JUST HURRY BACK. I ...UH... NEED TO GET THOSE APPLES TO EURYSTHEUS.
OF COURSE!
OF COURSE!

EVERY HOUR THAT HE STRAINED TO HOLD THE SKY FELT LIKE A YEAR TO HERCULES. HE WAS GLAD TO SEE THE TITAN RETURN.
HERE THEY ARE! VERY PRETTY. EURYSTHEUS WILL LIKE THEM.
YES, I THINK SO TOO. NOW, TAKE BACK THE SKY.
NO. NO, I THINK NOT. I HAVE HELD THE SKY FOR LONG ENOUGH. YOU CAN HOLD IT FROM NOW ON.
REMEMBER, I PROMISED TO BRING THE APPLES HERE. I NEVER SAID I WOULD TAKE BACK THE SKY.
WHAT?!?
DO NOT WORRY. I WILL TAKE THE APPLES TO EURYSTHEUS FOR YOU.
THANK YOU FOR THAT.
YOU HAVE BEEN HOLDING THE SKY MANY YEARS. I SUPPOSE IT IS ONLY FAIR THAT SOMEONE ELSE DO IT FOR A WHILE.
I WONDER IF YOU CAN DO ME A FAVOR, THOUGH?
CAN YOU TAKE BACK THE SKY FOR A TIME?
IF I FOLD MY CLOAK INTO A PAD FOR MY SHOULDERS I WOULD BE MORE COMFORTABLE.
HMMM. I SUPPOSE.
A PAD WOULD HAVE BEEN NICE ALL THOSE YEARS I WAS HOLDING THE SKY.

BE QUICK. THERE ARE MANY THINGS I WANT TO DO.
NO. NO, I THINK NOT. I ASKED YOU TO TAKE BACK THE SKY FOR A TIME. I NEVER SAID HOW LONG.
NOOOOOOO!!! THIS IS NOT FAIR! COME BACK!
HA! JUST AS FAIR AS YOU LEAVING ME TO DO YOUR WORK.
NOOOOOOOOOOOOOOOOOOOO

THERE, EURYSTHEUS. THE APPLES YOU DEMANDED.
MAGNIFICENT!
HERA WAS UPSET THAT ANYONE COULD GET THE APPLES THAT BELONGED TO HER. THAT HERCULES MANAGED IT, WHEN SHE HATED HIM SO MUCH, MADE HER FURIOUS.
SHE WAS DETERMINED TO FIND A TASK THAT HERCULES COULD NOT HOPE TO COMPLETE.
AH! I HAVE THE PERFECT TWELFTH LABOR FOR YOU, HERCULES.
YOU MUST GO INTO THE UNDERWORLD, THE LAND OF THE DEAD, AND BRING ME BACK THE THREE-HEADED GUARD DOG, CERBERUS!
I DOUBT HADES, THE GOD OF THE UNDERWORLD, WILL BE HAPPY WITH THAT.
THE ORACLE SENT YOU BY THE WILL OF THE GODS.
SURELY HADES WILL RESPECT THAT. NOW, GO!
NOT KNOWING WHAT ELSE TO DO, HERCULES TRAVELED TO THE RIVER STYX, WHERE THE BOATMAN CHARON FERRIES THE SOULS OF THE DEAD TO THE UNDERWORLD.
I SEEK PASSAGE TO THE REALM OF HADES.

YOU ARE NOT DEAD.
NO, BUT I MUST GO.
JUST KNOW THAT NO ONE RETURNS FROM THE UNDERWORLD. NOT UNLESS HADES LETS HIM GO.
I KNOW.
THE MONSTROUS CERBERUS, GUARDIAN OF THE GATES OF THE UNDERWORLD, MADE SURE THAT NO ONE ESCAPED BACK INTO THE LAND OF THE LIVING.
AS HERCULES PASSED BY, HE KNEW HE MIGHT NEVER SEE THE WORLD ABOVE AGAIN.
ALONG TWISTING PATHS, HE MADE HIS WAY TO THE COURT OF HADES, LORD OF THE DEAD.

AH. I KNEW THAT A LIVING MAN HAD ENTERED MY REALM, BUT I DID NOT REALIZE THAT IT WAS YOU.
WELCOME, SON OF MY BROTHER ZEUS. WHY ARE *YOU* HERE?
I COME BECAUSE THE ORACLE AT DELPHI PUT ME IN THE SERVICE OF EURYSTHEUS.
HE COMMANDED ME TO BRING HIM CERBERUS.
DID HE? I THINK I SEE HERA'S HAND IN THIS. SHE NEVER LIKED YOU. SHE THINKS I WILL NOT LET YOU GO.
BECAUSE OF THAT, AND BECAUSE I DO NOT WANT TO ANGER ZEUS, I THINK I WILL LET YOU RETURN TO THE LAND OF THE LIVING.
THANK YOU, GREAT HADES.
WILL YOU LET ME COMPLETE MY TASK? CAN I TAKE CERBERUS WITH ME?
SINCE YOU ARE OBEYING THE ORACLE, I WILL ALLOW YOU TO TAKE CERBERUS...
BUT ONLY IF YOU CAN TAME HIM WITH YOUR BARE HANDS.
OH, AND TELL EURYSTHEUS THAT YOUR SERVICE IS AT AN END. TELL HIM I SAID SO.
GRRRRRRRRRRRR

AAAARRRR!
RRRRRRRRRRRRRRRRRRR

KA-A-KATHOOM!
AAIIIEEEEE!
NOW, RETURN TO YOUR MASTER.
I HAVE COMPLETED THE TWELFTH LABOR YOU GAVE ME.
NOW MY SERVICE TO YOU IS FINISHED.
THAT WAS THE END OF THE TWELVE LABORS OF HERCULES, BUT THAT WAS NOT THE END OF HIS ADVENTURES.
ALL HIS LIFE, HERCULES NEVER STOPPED MAKING DANGEROUS JOURNEYS AND FIGHTING AGAINST FEARSOME ENEMIES, BUT THOSE ARE STORIES FOR ANOTHER TIME.

GLOSSARY

AMAZONS: a race of female warriors of Greek legend. Hippolyta, daughter of the god of war—Ares—is the queen of the Amazons.

ARTEMIS: the Greek goddess of the moon and of the hunt

BOAR: a male pig

HADES: the underground dwelling place of the dead in Greek mythology

HERA: the immortal wife of Zeus

HIDE: the skin of an animal

HIND: a female deer

IMMORTAL: a being that never dies

MARE: a female horse

MORTAL: a being that dies

NYMPH: in Greek mythology, goddesses of nature who are often represented as beautiful women living in the mountains, forests, trees, and waters

ORACLE: a priestess of ancient Greece through whom a god or gods were believed to speak

POSEIDON: the Greek god of the sea

TITAN: according to Greek mythology, a race of giants that ruled the earth before their overthrow by the Greek gods

ZEUS: king of the gods, father of Hercules

pencil from page 45

FURTHER READING AND WEBSITES

Greek Mythology: The Labors of Hercules
http://www.mythweb.com/hercules/index.html
With engaging cartoons and easy-to-read text, this kid-friendly site explores the labors of Hercules and also tells the stories of several other Greek heroes.

Hamilton, Edith. *Mythology*. New York: Warner Books, Inc., 1999.
First published in 1942, this classic work is a collection of lively retellings of Greek, Roman, and Norse tales.

Perseus Project: Hercules: Greece's Greatest Hero
http://www.perseus.tufts.edu/Herakles/index.html
This website from Tufts University in Massachusetts features a wealth of information about the legend of Hercules, including his twelve labors and other stories.

Philip, Neil. *Mythology*. New York: Dorling Kindersley, 1999.
This volume in the Eyewitness Books series uses dozens of colorful photos and illustrations to explore myths from around the world.

Roberts, Morgan J. *Classical Deities and Heroes*. New York: Metro Books, 1995.
Filled with colorful illustrations and photos of ancient artifacts, this book recounts many of the most popular Greek and Roman myths, including the twelve labors of Hercules.

Thomas Bulfinch: Bulfinch's Mythology
http://www.classicreader.com/booktoc.php/sid.2/bookid.2823/
This website features one of the most popular English-language compilations of ancient myths. This classic work, which includes many Greek myths, was compiled by American Thomas Bulfinch in the 1800s.

CREATING HERCULES: THE TWELVE LABORS

To create the story of Hercules' Twelve Labors, author Paul Storrie relied heavily on both Thomas Bulfinch's *The Age of Fable*, first published in 1859, and Edith Hamilton's *Mythology*, first published in 1942. Both of these drew their material from the work of ancient poets such as Ovid and Virgil. Artist Steve Kurth used numerous historical and traditional sources to give the art an authentic feel, from the classical Greek architecture to the clothing, weapons and armor worn by the characters. Together, the art and narrative text bring to life the mightiest hero of Greek myth, whose battles against gods and monsters earned him a place on Mt. Olympus, the home of the Greek gods.

INDEX

ABOUT THE AUTHOR AND THE ARTIST

PAUL D. STORRIE was born and raised in Detroit, Michigan and has returned to live there again and again after living in other cities and states. He began writing professionally in 1987 and has written comics for Caliber Comics, Moonstone Books, Marvel Comics and DC Comics. Some of the titles he's worked on include *Robyn of Sherwood*, featuring stories about Robin Hood's daughter, *Batman Beyond*, *Gotham Girls*, *Captain America: Red, White and Blue* and *Mutant X*.

STEVE KURTH was born and raised in west central Wisconsin. He graduated with a bachelor's degree in fine arts in illustration from the University Wisconsin at Eau Claire. Steve's art has appeared in numerous comic books, including *G.I. Joe*, *Micronauts*, *Ghostbusters*, *Dragonlance*, and *Cracked* magazine.